Category Theory in Programming

From Math to Code

Table of Contents

Chapter 1. Introduction

Special Report: "Category Theory in Programming: From Math to Code"

Welcome to a journey from abstract mathematics to everyday code in our special report on Category Theory in Programming. In a rapidly digitizing world, understanding these concepts can give you a competitive edge and unlock new possibilities in software design. This report starts by lightly introducing the complex mathematical system called 'category theory,' renowned for its high level of abstraction, and gradually descends into its tangible applications in programming. Our carefully crafted report ensures that complex ideas are broken down into digestible concepts, making it an enlightening read not merely for mathematicians and programmers, but for anyone drawn towards the intriguing interface of mathematics and computer science. Discover how category theory extends its roots deep into programming, enhancing problem-solving strategies, and how it's shaping the future of code creation. Buckle up as we explore this exciting path from math to code!

Chapter 2. Introduction to Category Theory

Category theory is a branch of mathematics that, despite its reputation for being abstract and difficult to grasp, serves as a versatile tool applicable to various areas of logical and mathematical disciplines. In the realm of computer science, category theory's principles have demonstrated profound repercussions on structuring code, designing software, and approaching data-orientated challenges. To appreciate its significance and potential, we must first understand what category theory is and what it entails.

2.1. A Snapshot of Category Theory

In essence, category theory studies structures and their relations. It is less concerned with the details of objects and more focused on the relationships and transformations between these structures. Precisely, it delves into the architecture of mathematical structures and interactions. Its main actors are objects and morphisms (also called arrows or maps). The latter represents relations or transitions between objects.

You might be familiar with set theory, a branch of mathematical logic that studies sets, or collections of objects. Category theory could be viewed as a step away from this type of reasoning as it zooms out to focus on how these sets (objects) are connected (via morphisms). It serves as a bridge, enabling mathematicians and scientists to jump from one concept to another, fostering relationships between traditionally isolated fields.

2.2. Objects and Morphisms

In other mathematical systems, such as set theory, properties and elements define objects. However, in category theory, the focus shifts onto the morphisms that link objects. These morphisms, as mentioned earlier, represent transitions or maps between objects.

Morphisms obey two simple rules: they can be composed (you can go from object A to B, then B to C via two morphisms), and they have identities (there is always a morphism from object A to itself). It's interesting to note that these two rules in category theory encapsulate concepts found in programming: for example, identity maps to the concept of the identity function, and composition corresponds to function composition.

The simplicity of these rules and their elemental but universal nature provides category theory its extensive applicability and power to bring together diverse mathematical areas under one roof.

2.3. Categories

A category comprises objects and morphisms. Importantly, it follows the rules of morphism composition and identity. In the realm of set theory, you could envision a category where sets are objects and functions are morphisms.

Any area of mathematics that involves objects and structured relations among them lays down a fertile ground for seeing categories in action. Topology, with its topological spaces and continuous functions, or group theory, with its groups and group homomorphisms, provide insightful examples of this.

2.4. Functors

Functors, the next essential concept in category theory, conduct a critical role in establishing links between categories. You can perceive a functor as a mechanism that transports concepts from one category to another while preserving their structure. It maps objects in one category to another and morphisms similarly in a way that respects their compositional structure.

The role of functors can be transformative: not simply being a bridge but often offering a new insightful perspective or revealing hidden patterns, thereby enriching the understanding of both categories involved and the underlying mathematics.

These structural-preserving mappings resonate with the mappings in programming. In object-oriented programming, for instance, classes and methods can be linked to category theory's objects and morphisms, while interfaces resemble functors.

2.5. Natural Transformations

Yet another pivotal theory, natural transformations, describe maps between functors. They provide a way to morph or transform one functor into another while keeping their connection with the original categories intact. As complex as they may sound, natural transformations embody a sensible and intuitive concept: changes that preserve structure and relationships are 'natural' changes.

Unsurprisingly, natural transformations have found an echo in the programming world within the idea of refactoring, where code is altered without changing its outward behavior or the program's overall outcome.

2.6. Why Category Theory in Programming?

While this mathematical system may seem abstract and daunting, its principles can be all more valuable when grasped. In programming, it enhances code reliability, modularity, and expressiveness. It provides useful metaphors and jargon that can streamline the discourse about program structure and design.

Moreover, embracing category theory can solidify the understanding of functional programming principles, laying the groundwork for cleaner, more maintainable, efficient, and side-effect free code. Many principles in functional programming languages like Haskell or Scala have their roots in category theory.

In the upcoming sections, we will delve deeper into category theory's numerous concepts, its intersections with the sphere of programming, and how each shapes the other. We will discover the power of the abstractions that category theory provides and explore how these abstractions can be wielded to design and grapple better with the intricate challenges in the ever-evolving field of programming. Get ready for an exciting exploration into the mathematical underpinnings of code!

Chapter 3. Principles and Concepts of Category Theory

Before digging deep into the principles and concepts of category theory, it's essential to understand its very foundation - Mathematics. Category theory is a branch of abstract mathematics that deals with structures and their relationships. Being highly theoretical, an understanding of certain mathematical concepts is worthwhile for grasping it.

3.1. Set Theory

The bedrock of many mathematical concepts, including category theory, is set theory. A 'set' is a collection of distinct objects, known as 'elements.' These elements may well represent anything - numbers, people, letters, or even other sets. If an object 'a' belongs to a set 'A,' it is denoted as 'a ⬚ A.' Set theory provides basis of mathematical reasoning and sheds light on the understanding of functions - a key component in category theory.

3.2. Functions and their Anatomy

In its essence, a function is a relationship where an input is related to an output. In the context of sets, if we have two sets, say, 'A' and 'B,' and every element of 'A' (input) corresponds to at least one element of 'B' (output), this relationship is called a function. Notably, in category theory, functions are referred to as 'morphisms' or 'arrows,' and sets are termed as 'objects.'

3.3. Categories: The Building Blocks

A 'Category,' C, in the simplest terms, can be regarded as a collection of 'objects' and 'arrows' between them, following specific rules. Objects could represent anything, let it be numbers, shapes, data types, or data structures, while arrows signify the relationship between these objects. Each arrow has a 'domain' (from where it starts) and 'codomain' (where it ends).

The two rules for any category are:

1. For every object 'A,' there exists an 'identity morphism' that maps 'A' to itself. This is denoted as id_A, essentially meaning that if you start and end at an object 'A', you remain at 'A'.

2. Arrows or morphisms must be 'composable.' Given two arrows, f: A→B and g: B→C, there must exist a third arrow, say h = g o f, that goes directly from A to C (f followed by g).

This seemingly straightforward concept is what serves as a cornerstone of category theory.

3.4. From Abstract to Concrete: Examples of Categories

Let's narrow down from the abstract concept of categories to more tangible examples. A prevalent example in the world of mathematics is the category 'Set,' which includes all sets as objects and all functions between those sets as morphisms. Another example is 'Pos,' the category of all partially ordered sets (or posets) where morphisms are order-preserving maps.

In the realm of computer science, consider 'Hask' (a simplified theoretical model of Haskell's type system) where objects are Haskell types, and morphisms are functions in Haskell.

3.5. Morphism Types and Role

Morphisms aren't limited to being just functions. There are three special types of morphisms—Monomorphism, Epimorphism, and Isomorphism, shaping the structure further:

- Monomorphism: A morphism f: A→B is a monomorphism if it preserves distinctness. If arrows g1, g2: B→A exist such that f * g_1 = f * g_2, then g_1 = g_2.

- Epimorphism: A morphism f: A → B is an epimorphism if it is surjective i.e., for every 'b' in B, there exists at least one 'a' in A such that f(a) = b.

- Isomorphism: It is a special kind of morphism that has an inverse. If there are two objects 'A' and 'B' and a morphism f: A → B, then 'f' is an isomorphism if there exists a morphism g: B → A such that f * g = id_A and g * f = id_B.

These types of morphisms add more flexibility and depth to the relationships between objects, opening up a new world of possibilities.

3.6. Functors: The Transformers

Functors exist as an extension of morphisms, ensuring the transformation from one category to another while preserving the structures of objects (or hardly changing them). If you have two categories, say, 'C' and 'D', a functor 'F' maps each object in 'C' to an object in 'D' and each morphism in 'C' to a morphism in 'D' without compromising the identity and composition rules.

Over the years, category theory has grown beyond its mathematical foundation. Engineers, computer scientists, and even philosophers identify it as a language for connecting disparate fields, fortifying them by injecting a higher level of reasoning and abstraction. By understanding this, we can appreciate the transition of these theoretical constructs into tangible implements in programming.

Chapter 4. Object and Morphism: The Building Blocks

In the world of abstract mathematics, two simple yet powerful constructs form the genesis of category theory: objects and morphisms. Ensconced in the fortified walls of realms much beyond our pondering, these entities rest side-by-side, defining the very core of the mystical land that is category theory. Let's unfurl the pages and comprehend the nature of these engrossing entities.

4.1. The Essence of Objects

Objects in category theory, unlike the objects encountered in object-oriented programming, are considerably abstract. They hold no properties or characteristics that could be scaled down to simpler elements. An object may represent a set, a group, a topological space, or a multitude of other mathematical structures, depending on the specific category in which they reside. However, beyond this, an object remains a closed book. It does not entertain queries related to its internal structure or elements.

```
`\`

    Consider this simply: In category theory, "objects
exist."
`\`
```

In quintessence, we always refer to objects concerning their interactions with other objects in their shared cosmos - that is, via morphisms.

4.2. Morphisms: Catalysts of Interaction

If objects furnish a skeletal framework for category theory, morphisms serve as the tendons and muscles, linking the objects together. The allure of morphisms resides in revealing the underlying relationships between disparate or alike objects. Morphisms may take the form of functions, maps or operators, depending on the nature of the category. They are the verbs breathing life into the sentence where objects are the subjects and objects. We will often find ourselves concerned with these entities in comparison, composition, and especially in their relation with objects.

4.2.1. The Grains of Comparison: The Hom-Set

Typically, it's not the individuality of morphisms that's intriguing but its relative group personality. In category theory, we tend to discuss morphisms in the context of hom-sets. To put this across in simple terms, a hom-set refers to the collection of all morphisms "from A to B" in a particular category, where A and B are objects of the same category. Keep note, 'set,' in a hom-set doesn't necessarily imply the collection is a set in formal set theory terms.

```
    For example, take a category 'Top' of topological
spaces.
    In this category, the hom-set "Hom(X, Y)" refers to
the
    collection of continuous functions from space X to
Y.
```

4.3. The Art of Composition

In the still-life painting of category theory, objects and morphisms are the major elements — the fruits and wine bottle, so to speak. However, it would be incomplete if it weren't for the light that envelops the model and confers upon it a semblance of life. This light is the composition of morphisms.

4.3.1. Composition: The Guiding Light

Morphisms depict links, communication lines, or relationships between objects. The composition of morphisms represents the cascading of these links, forming a network of interactions. In simple terms, if you have a link from object A to B and another from B to C, you can create a composite link from A to C directly. The significant part here is, it doesn't matter how you move from A to C (direct or indirect), the outcome (the composite morphism) remains the same.

> So, if "f" is a morphism from A to B, and "g" is a morphism
> from B to C, then their composition, denoted as "g ⬚ f,"
> is a morphism from A to C. It intrinsic in its definition
> that "h ⬚ (g ⬚ f) = (h ⬚ g) ⬚ f" -- the axiom of associativity.

> The idea of composition is fundamentally thread weaving through the entire tapestry of category theory,
> imparting a rich structure to sets of objects and their interactions. This concept also reflects in programming when consolidating complex systems from smaller functions, mirroring the abstraction and modular design in programming practices.

=== The King's decree: Rules Governing the Land

All kingdoms have their rules, and category theory is no
exception. To ensure harmony between objects, morphisms,
and their compositions, the theory adheres to a set of
laws: associativity and identity. These axioms play a
pivotal role, marking the demarcation between an
abstract category and mayhem.

==== The Law of Associativity

Imagine a sequence of morphisms, one morphism leading to
the next object and there to another through another
morphism. In theory, you can make a composite morphism
directly from the starting object to the ending object.
The order in which you club the morphisms together to
create this composite doesn't matter. This non-
dependency on parenthesization is the law of
associativity.

```
    A practical example presents itself in programming
as function
    composition. If you need to apply a sequence of
functions,
    the outcome does not depend on the order of
application.
```

==== The Rule of Identity

Each object in the category has an identity morphism
that maps the object back to itself. It has a neutral
impact, meaning any morphism composed with this identity
morphism remains the same.

```
\ \ \
```
    Think of it as the number one in multiplication.
Multiplying
    any number with one leaves the number unchanged.
Here, the
    identity morphism is your 'one,' and the
multiplication is your composition.
```
\ \ \
```

The laws of associativity and identity, ostensibly
basic, maintain the orderly interaction of objects and
prevent the kingdom of category theory from plunging
into chaos. They serve as the backbone, sustaining the
structure of category theory and regulating the conduct
of objects and morphisms.

Such are the building blocks that construct the universe
of category theory. From their premises arise the
fascinating structures and processes, illuminating the
journey ahead into the arcane intertwining of abstract
mathematics and code. The profound comprehension of
these elements and their rules sets the foundation for a
deeper exploration into how category theory is
streamlining programming, unlocking sophisticated
functionality with increased simplicity and abstraction.

Chapter 5. Functors: Connecting Categories

In the mathematical universe, a functor serves a transport medium, carrying objects and morphisms from one category to another while preserving their structure. As programmers, we can think of functors as a context, a programming construct, that allows operations on wrapped values preserving the original structure.

5.1. Mapping Categories via Functors

The concept of functors emerged from the domain of Category Theory. In essence, a functor is a special kind of map between categories. It is a structure-preserving mechanism which maintains the integrity of objects and morphisms that link them whenever they shift from one category to another. A functor 'F: C → D' takes each object 'X' from category 'C' and maps it to an object 'F(X)' in category 'D'. Similarly, a morphism 'f: X→Y' in 'C' is mapped to a morphism 'F(f): F(X)→F(Y)' in 'D'. The structure preservation property makes sure that for each composition 'g o f' in 'C', 'F(g o f) = F(g) o F(f)' holds true in the 'D'.

Functors, when applied in programming, encapsulate values within a context or computational effect. They allow programmers to perform operations on these encapsulated values while preserving the structure of original data.

Remember, in programming, 'Functor' is a typeclass or interface. Any type implementing this interface can be considered a functor. For instance, in Haskell, the class 'Functor' is defined for types which implement the fmap function. This function takes a function and a functor, applies the function inside the functor context, and returns a functor.

5.2. From Category Theory to Code

The word 'functor' in programming originated from the concept of functors in math. But how does this highly abstract concept find its use within our code?

Well, the abstract scenario of 'transforming objects and morphisms from one category to another' translates to a realistic coding scenario where 'data types are transformed using functions, while preserving the data type structure.' In other words, a functor provides a way for you to apply a function to a value inside a context or computational effect.

In effect, functors transpose the abstract mathematical idea to practical programming. We apply the concept of functors, for instance, when we use the 'map' function. If we have an array (a functor) of integers and a function that transforms integers, using 'map,' we can apply that function to every integer inside the array. The result is a new array (functor) of transformed integers while preserving the array structure.

5.3. Functor Laws

There are a couple of laws, known as the Functor Laws, which must be obeyed by every valid functor in the programming world.

- **Identity Law:** When we map the identity function over a functor, the functor that we get back should be the same as the original functor. In code: `fmap id == id`
- **Composition Law:** Mapping two composed functions over a functor should be the same as first mapping one function, and

then mapping the other. In code: `fmap (g . f) == fmap g . fmap f`

These laws preserve the structure and ensure the consistency of operations while dealing with functors.

5.4. Understanding Functors With Practical Examples

Let's consider a real-world example of functors by using the JavaScript programming language. In JavaScript, Array is an in-built functor. Let's use Array's map method (which is a functor method) to apply some function to the values inside the Array.

```javascript
let arr = [1, 2, 3, 4]; // Our Functor (Array)
let addOne = x => x + 1; // Our function

let arr2 = arr.map(addOne); // Apply the function to
elements in the Functor

console.log(arr2); // [2, 3, 4, 5]
```

In the given example, we have effortlessly applied the 'addOne' function to each element within the Array functor, generating an Array of transformed values as a result. The Array structure remains intact, pointing to the fact that the Array functor in JavaScript obeys the functor laws.

5.5. Conclusion

As we walk down the memory lane of Category Theory, with the semantics of Mathematics and the pragmatism of Programming holding our hands, we discover myriad treasures that enrich our programming style and enable us to build more error-free and maintainable code. Functors, these all-powerful structure-preserving transformers, hold a unique significance in this adventurous journey. Armed with the understanding of functors, you have added a potent tool to your mathematical knowledge and programming skills!

Next time you find yourself wishing for a way to apply a function to a computational context, reach for the nearest functor, & remember that this powerful and incredibly useful concept comes straight from the pages of Category Theory, bridging the gap between mathematical abstraction & tangible code. Here's to more structure, abstract thinking, and elegant code!

Chapter 6. Natural Transformations: Relating Functors

Before diving into the heart of natural transformations, it's worth acknowledging a key fact: category theory is thoroughly centered around relationships. Just as functors create a relationship between categories, natural transformations establish a relationship between functors. It's this consistently relational structure that surprises many newcomers to the field, but also underlies much of its practical power.

6.1. Understanding Natural Transformations

To start, a natural transformation provides a way to 'move' or 'map' one functor to another while preserving the structure. If you have two functors 'F' and 'G' going from a category 'C' to a category 'D', a natural transformation 'η' from 'F' to 'G' comprises of a family of morphisms in 'D' that satisfies certain coherence conditions.

Formally, for every object 'X' in 'C', there's a morphism 'ηX: FX → GX' in 'D'. These 'ηX' are called the component of η at 'X'.

If we picked two objects "A" and "B" and a morphism "f: A → B" in "C", then the diagram below indicates the naturality square:

```
          F(A) ---F(f)--> F(B)
           |               |
   ηA      |               | ηB
           V               V
```

```
        G(A) ---G(f)--> G(B)
```

The "naturality condition" states that for every morphism "f: A → B" in "C", the diagram must commute. This means that starting from any node, any path to another node is equivalent, regardless of the route taken. In layman's terms, the transformation is 'natural' in the sense that it doesn't rely on any specific feature of its category 'C'; it is organically coherent.

6.2. Natural Transformations in a Programming Context

So how does this flow into the realms of programming? Natural transformations find their use in refactorings of software, which are transformations of code that preserve code behavior.

Consider 'F' and 'G' as two implementations of an ADT (Abstract Data Type) represented as categories. A transformation from 'F' to 'G' that qualifies to be natural could be viewed as a methodology of changing one implementation to another while preserving the data interactions defined by the ADT.

Another example of naturally occurring transformations in programming languages is when moving from a concrete data type to an abstract one. For instance, let's consider a List and an Optional (or Maybe in Haskell); both can be Functors. A Natural Transformation can be a function that goes from a List of A to Maybe A taking the possibly present first element of the list.

6.3. Natural Isomorphism

As we're gaining familiarity with these concepts, it might be tempting to ask whether there could be a kind of 'inverse' to natural transformations. And indeed, there's something called a 'natural isomorphism.'

A natural isomorphism is a natural transformation that is also an isomorphism in the category of functors from 'C' to 'D'. In other words, a natural transformation 'η: F → G' is a natural isomorphism if for all objects 'X' in 'C', the morphism 'ηX' is an isomorphism in 'D'. The presence of such natural isomorphisms is a strong indication about the 'sameness' of the two functors.

6.4. Conclusion

Dissecting natural transformations illuminates one of the key ideas of category theory: creating and analyzing relationships between structures. Just like functors impose structure upon categories, natural transformations give structure to functors. This characteristic of reflecting levels of abstraction keeps unfolding in category theory, providing programmers with an additional toolbox for tackling complex software challenges. In such ways, it opens up avenues for not only improved code creation but also mindful refactoring.

It's important, along with learning the theoretical aspects of category theory, to also recognize and appreciate its programmatic applications, since these suggest that there's more to coding than just writing lines of instructions. Yes, they're powerful tools, engines of abstraction, but they are also part of the greater discourse in the field of mathematics, a testament to its ubiquity and infinite applicability. Understanding these elements may pave the way to becoming not only a proficient programmer, but a conscientious one, always seeking the ideal balance between abstraction and implementation, theory and practice. This synergy is what natural transformations, and indeed category theory as a whole, present to the mindful programmer.

Chapter 7. Monads in Category Theory: Powerful Abstraction

As prevalent as these monads may be in category theory, the name can be misleading. One might infer that they're a type of mathematical entity, such as a monoid or a number. However, monads are actually a type of structure that can be instituted within category theory. Think of it as a blueprint that provides a method of structuring computations. Monads equivocate computations into categories, in turn, making them amenable for manipulation and reasoning with the mighty tools of category theory.

7.1. Understanding the Basics

Let's commence by understanding the basic terminologies of monads in category theory.

In category theory, a monad is a type of functor, a mapping between categories. A monad T associates every object X in the category C to an object T(X)" in C. It further connects every morphism f: X → Y in C to a morphism T(f): T(X) → T(Y) in C. This operation preserves the identity morphisms and composition of morphisms.

But, a monad T consists of not just the functor component but also comprises two essential natural transformations too. One is η (Eta), a transformation that associates every object X in C to a morphism η_X: X → T(X), and μ (Mu), a transformation that associates every object X in C to a morphism μ_X: T(T(X)) → T(X). These transformations must satisfy a set of laws known as the Monad laws. The combination of the functor T with the transformations η and μ respecting the Monad laws forms the monad.

7.2. Monad Laws

Monad laws in category theory ensure the consistent function of monads. They are the axioms of monads, obligating the fulfillment of these laws for any construction to be a valid monad. Monad laws include:

1. Left Identity: η followed by μ is the same as the identity function. Mathematically, $\mu \cdot T(\eta) = id$.

2. Right Identity: η followed by μ is the same as the identity function. Mathematically, $\mu \cdot \eta T = id$.

3. Associativity: μ followed by μ = $T(\mu)$ followed by μ.

These laws ensure that μ and η work harmoniously and aid the organizing of computations, looping, conditional execution, and error handling in an algebraic sense.

7.3. Monads in Programming

Programming languages often incorporate the theory of monads allowing developers to incorporate side effects, such as state or I/O, into their purely functional programs. Monads also provide a unified, composable model for different kinds of computations (e.g. exception handling, state, and I/O).

One of the most popular languages that deeply integrates monads is Haskell. In Haskell, a monad is a typeclass, a type system construct that supports polymorphism. It incorporates three components namely, 'return', '>>=' (bind), and '>>' to manage and carry functionality. It's worth noting that the 'return' function in the Monads of Haskell equivocates to the η of category theory and '>>=' equivocates to μ.

For example, the Maybe Monad in Haskell allows computations to fail gracefully and manage 'null' values, saving us from Null pointer error.

```
data Maybe a = Nothing | Just a
instance Monad Maybe

return x = Just x

Nothing >>= func = Nothing
Just val >>= func  = func val
```

The bind operation "(>>=)" passes the context (in this case, the possibility of failure) to the next computation. From the way it's defined, if the computation has already failed (i.e. we are dealing with Nothing), then it "short-circuits" and automatically provides a failing computation. If the computation is successful, then we merely apply the function.

Leveraging this monadic structure, we can chain calculations that may fail, which will only continue as long as every step succeeds.

7.4. Conclusion: The Power of Monads

Monads, hence grant a powerful abstraction in functional programming. They enable the encapsulation of computational context – be it state, I/O, exception handling, or something else – into a composable, declarative format. Programmers can then write robust, side-effect-free code in a high-level declarative style without worrying about the underlying complexities of state management or I/O.

While this brief introduction to the theory of monads in programming only scratches the surface of the topic, it provides insight into how a rather abstract concept from applied mathematics can have profound implications on the practice of writing software. As the fields of mathematics and computer science continue to intertwine and evolve, the role of structures like monads will undoubtedly continue to expand.

Chapter 8. Category Theory's Leap to Programming

Let's commence our journey by understanding what category theory is. For centuries, mathematicians have devised structures to encapsulate mathematical concepts - sets, groups, vectors, and topologies, to name a few. However, what if there was an even more abstract way to capture these concepts? Category theory is that level of abstraction, a unifying umbrella underneath which all these structures sit.

8.1. What is Category Theory?

Category theory, at its core, is a mathematical discipline focused on abstraction, transformation, and composition. Originally developed in the mid-20th century as a means of connecting different branches of mathematics, it defines a language that universally translates between different mathematical structures.

A **category** in category theory is composed of **objects** and **arrows** (also commonly known as **morphisms**). While objects encompass little more than an abstract existence, morphisms establish relationships and transitions between these objects. The three principles that distinguish category theory are:

1. Composition: Morphisms can be composed, reminiscent of stringing together functions in programming. If we have an arrow from object A to B and another from B to C, by composition, we have another arrow from A to C.

2. Associativity: The way morphisms compose doesn't depend on the grouping. If there are morphisms from A to B, B to C, and C to D, you can move from A to D via B and C, regardless of whether you move from A to C first then C to D or A to B and then B to D.

3. Identity: Every object has an identity morphism. This loops from an object back to itself and is analogous to the number one in multiplication or the Boolean 'true' in logical operations.

8.2. Category Theory and Programming: The Connection

Now, let's head towards the exciting part: How does category theory crossover into programming? The leap from mathematical category theory to programming might seem abstract in itself, but once we bridge this gap, it opens a universe of possibilities.

Programs are mathematical objects: they have structure and obey specific rules, equivalent to the objects and morphisms in category theory. Consider functions, the building blocks of programming. They capture transformation from one set of data to another - precisely how morphisms relate objects.

Interestingly, the concept of composition is fundamental in both category theory and programming. Software developers are familiar with composing small functions to form more complicated structures - loosely synonymous with the composition of morphisms. Not convinced yet? Let's take the higher-order function that takes other functions as arguments or returns them as results. It closely mirrors the morphism composition concept.

8.3. Category Theory's Influence on Functional Programming

It would be remiss to talk about category theory in programming without discussing its influence on the functional programming paradigm. Functional programming languages like Haskell, Scala, or F# draw heavily from category theory concepts. But why? One reason is the shared philosophy between category theory and functional languages: both value the composition and interaction of parts over changing internal states.

Moreover, the mathematics embraced within category theory provides a framework within which to analyze and reason about our code. This, in turn, allows for the design of APIs and libraries with more predictable behavior, making code safer and easier to maintain.

Another key concept brought in by category theory is **functors**. In programming, a functor is an object or function that can be used with a map function. This concept is fundamental in functional programming languages, as the map function and functors work in unison to manipulate data without mutating state, concurrent with the principles of functional programming.

8.4. The Future of Category Theory in Programming

Despite its theoretical backbone, category theory offers very tangible benefits for programming, particularly in structuring and scaling code. Its ability to connect different areas and concepts provides a scaffolding that spans across disciplines and promotes more robust and adaptable logic.

Developers can leverage the predictability engraved in category theory for software maintenance and upgrading, enabling the creation of more scalable, reliable, and safer software applications. In turn, the mathematical rigor brought into programming can yield optimized solutions and innovate development practices.

Furthermore, category theory is becoming an essential tool for many cutting-edge fields, like quantum computing, where the emphasis is on transformations and morphisms as in categories.

Though not a silver bullet, category theory is steadily gaining ground as a valuable tool for solving complex programming problems. That said, the adoption of abstract mathematical concepts depends on the willingness of developers to bend traditional approaches. As programming continues to grow and evolve, expect category theory to play a more significant role in its future journey.

In conclusion, category theory allows us to see the world from a higher vantage point. It's a challenging, abstract, and labyrinthine realm. However, entering this maze introduces one to a new way of viewing problems, enabling us to refactor and distill them to their most universal forms. Category theory is an essential leap to broader and better understanding programming in its purest essence.

Chapter 9. Understanding Programming Through Category Theory

Category theory, with its abstract forms and robust concepts, isn't the easiest of topics to understand, let alone apply in a different domain like programming. That being said, it provides a formidable mathematical framework that, when grasped properly, has the potential to revolutionize your programming approach.

9.1. The Basics

First, let's briefly touch upon what category theory is. Category theory is a branch of mathematics that deals with mathematical structures and their relationships. In essence, it helps in understanding the structure of mathematical models by emphasizing the relationships between different elements, rather than focusing on their individual traits.

In the context of category theory, you'll often encounter two fundamental entities: objects and arrows (also known as morphisms). The objects are usually abstract mathematical structures (like sets, groups, and rings) and the arrows denote relationships or processes between these objects.

A typical category has multiple objects and arrows, paired in a way that any two arrows with a common object can "compose" to form a larger structure retaining the essence of its components. This 'composition' also forms a critical part of the category theory, where the focus is primarily on relationships and their compositions, not entities in isolation.

9.2. Grasping Morphisms

As we inclined previously, in category theory, the focus is on the arrows, i.e., morphisms. Unlike traditional mathematical disciplines, it's not so much about what the objects 'are' but how they relate.

Morphisms stand for relationships or transformations from one object to another. They embody all you need to know about the structure in a respective category. From a programming perspective, consider morphisms analogous to functions.

9.3. Composition

If there's one thing you can't miss about category theory, it's composition. Morphisms (or arrows) in a category follow specific rules of combination known as 'composition'. Given two morphisms, say 'f' and 'g', if 'f' has an endpoint where 'g' starts (also known as a common 'domain'), these two can compose to give a new entity 'g.f'.

Notably, composition obeys two main rules: Associativity and the existence of Identity morphisms. Associativity deals with the sequence of compositions – if you have three morphisms 'f', 'g', and 'h' that can be composed, their association doesn't matter. In other words, (h.g).f is the same as h.(g.f).

Identity morphism, on the other hand, is a special morphism associated with each object in a category, which when composed with any morphism associated with the same object results in the same unaltered morphism.

9.4. Programming as a Category

At this juncture, one might wonder, "What does all this abstraction have to do with programming?"

Well, categories, objects, and morphisms have direct parallels in the world of programming. A programming language forms a category where objects can be understood as types, and morphisms represent functions. Suppose we have a type 'A' and another type 'B'. A function 'f' that transforms 'A' to 'B' can be considered a morphism mapping object 'A' to object 'B'.

Similarly, the notion of 'composition', which is fundamental to category theory, is prevalent in programming. When we invoke a function with the result of another function, we are implementing 'composition'. If you've ever piped commands in respective programming languages, you have engaged with composition.

9.5. Identity Functions and Isomorphisms

The concept of Identity morphisms in category theory has precise counterparts in programming, known as identity functions. As in category theory, an identity function, when called with any other function, leaves the function and its result unaltered. It is the Neutral Element for function composition.

Furthermore, the idea of Isomorphisms in category theory has valuable implications in programming. When there exist two morphisms between two objects in a category such that they can 'reverse' each other under composition, we say an isomorphism exists between the objects.

In programming, two types can be considered isomorphic if we can find two functions that can convert back and forth between the types without losing information. An appreciation of such Isomorphisms can lead to a clearer, more natural expression of program logic.

9.6. Functor: Elevating Functions

Functors are another fundamental concept in category theory that can be beneficial for programmers. A functor maps a category to another while maintaining the original category's structure. It's akin to a 'function of types and functions'.

In practicality, functors are used widely in functional programming, often seen in the context of data types being transformed by functions. They help to encapsulate data manipulation in a context, preventing unwanted side effects.

In conclusion, understanding programming through the lens of category theory can offer a fresh perspective. As we've seen, its abstract principles can have tangible and efficient applications in code. However, don't fret if it feels overwhelming to begin with—like any good programming paradigm, the benefits will become more evident with experience and practice. Consider this an open invitation to explore the fascinating conjunction of abstract mathematics and practical coding!

Chapter 10. Category Theory in Practice: Application in Modern Programming Languages

Category theory, at first, might seem detached from the practical world of programming, lost in a maze of abstract mathematics. However, it deeply intertwines with the essence of many modern programming languages and their constructs. It encapsulates universal concepts seen in different lingos and libraries, presenting an opportunity to understand programming at a more comprehensive level.

Set up your workstations and let's embark on this enlightening deep-dive into the practical aspects of category theory in modern programming languages.

10.1. Monad: The Mathematical Structure in Functional Programming

Monads, a concept arising from category theory, permeate functional programming languages. Haskell, for instance, uses Monads extensively as a mechanism for sequencing operations. A Monad in Haskell is a type class with two fundamental functions: bind (>>=) and return.

```
class Monad m where
    (>>=) :: m a -> (a -> m b) -> m b
```

```
return :: a -> m a
```

`return` wraps a value into a monadic type, while `bind` serves to feed a monadic value into a function that returns another monadic value. By sequencing operations, monads provide a way of handling state, side effects, exceptions, and computation flow.

10.2. Programming Paradigms and Category Theory

In software engineering, there's a constant need to explore new paradigms, which often means incorporating concepts from formal mathematics to better capture programming abstractions. Category theory, being "a theory of functions," naturally synergizes with functional programming languages like Haskell, Scala, or Erlang.

For example, Scala uses Functors, a concept rooted in category theory. In Scala, Functors are used to map one category (a) to another (b) using a function `f`.

```
trait Functor[F[_]] {
  def map[A, B](fa: F[A])(f: A => B): F[B]
}
```

10.3. Categorical Frameworks: Arrow, Applicative, and Beyond

Beyond Monads and Functors, categorical concepts such as Arrow and Applicative play essential roles too.

Arrows, used heavily in Haskell, extend the base monad concept, providing more control over monadic computations. They're typically leveraged for computations that contain static structures.

```
class Arrow a where
    arr :: (b -> c) -> a b c
    (>>>) :: a b c -> a c d -> a b d
    first :: a b c -> a (b,d) (c,d)
```

Applicatives, on the other hand, assist when a sequence of actions needs to be combined over time. They sit between Functors and Monads, providing an essential tool for abstracting control flow in computations.

```
class (Functor f) => Applicative f where
    pure :: a -> f a
    (<*>) :: f (a -> b) -> f a -> f b
```

These constructs, arising from category theory, allow programmers to describe complex computations in a simple, elegant, and abstract manner.

10.4. Leveraging Category Theory for Software Design

Category theory has also been applied to influence the design of software. For instance, the concept of type classes in Haskell is influenced by the categorical construct of a "class." In C++, template metaprogramming mirrors category-theoretic principles.

Arguably, these design approaches guided by category theory lead to more extensible, modular, and maintainable codebases.

10.5. Toward the Future: Higher-Order Theories and Polyglot Programming

As the software world propels towards higher-order theories and polyglot programming, the underlying concepts provided by category theory help build a vibrant toolkit for developers, facilitating a deeper understanding of their craft.

Category theory does not just influence the languages we use today; it shapes the future of programming itself, offering a powerful framework for examining and creating new programming languages.

Despite the steep learning curve, investing in understanding category theory guarantees leveled-up problem-solving skills, offering a broader perspective on the intricate world of code, being another vibrant example of the interplay between mathematics and programming.

10.6. Conclusion

The exploration of these complex ideas brings us back full circle to the fundamental symbiosis of programming and mathematics, with category theory sitting at the heart of this relationship. It transcends beyond abstract theories and mathematical titling, influencing the way we approach programming, offering a rich and broad context to modern programming languages and practices, and shaping the horizon of our programming future.

Implementing category theory concepts in your programming practices goes beyond syntactic sugar; it's more about turning toward fundamentally sound principles drawn from formal mathematics to guide our code, programs, and systems. Bringing categories from theoretical mathematics to your IDE can seem formidable, but for those willing to unlock this new paradigm, there are immense rewards to reap.

After all, the further we push into novel realms of programming, the more we find the echoes of abstract mathematics guiding the way, with category theory playing a central role. It's not just the theory of categories, but it's becoming the theoretical backbone of programming itself.

Chapter 11. Future Perspectives: Category Theory in Programming

As we usher in the era of technologies such as machine learning, data science, quantum computing, and functional programming, the role of category theory in programming is becoming increasingly crucial. This mathematical framework has been reshaping the perspective of encoding, thereby providing a common ground that bridges different domains of software design.

11.1. The Adaptive Nature of Category Theory

Category theory isn't a new kid on the mathematical block. It was originally conceived to unify disparate fields within mathematics and has demonstrated its efficacy in achieving this objective remarkably well. However, when we transpose this theory into the programming realm, we witness its true adaptability come alive. Here, it becomes an abstract structure that visualizes disparate data types and functions, the DNA of any coding language, as objects and morphisms respectively. The comprehension of these fundamental software properties through the sophisticated lenses of category theory opens up innovative pathways for coding design and optimization.

Invoking category theory in programming does not necessitate a change in the coding language. Instead, it provides an alternative perspective, allowing developers to view their logical structures under a new light of universality and scalability. By emphasizing composability, category theory allows greater reusability of code.

11.2. Category Theory Driving Computational Learning Theory

Category theory also extends its prowess to the world of machine learning and artificial intelligence. In the expanding field of computational learning theory, the role of category theory becomes increasingly recognized as a unifying force. It aids the thought process of machine learning design by eliciting the similar foundational concepts of universal properties and morphism.

The essence of machine learning revolves around data transformation; data is regularly transfigured and given birth anew as useful insights and predictions. It is here that category theory, with its unique perspective on functions (morphisms), distinguishes itself. The concept of functors extending from categories promotes the concept of lifting operations to function over data, ensuring that the integrity of the computational structure remains intact. This allows developers to manage complex data transformations with increased grace and simplicity.

11.3. Functional Programming: A New Frontier

Functional programming is another field where category theory is particularly influential. It's common to think that learning functional programming implies obtaining proficiency in languages like Haskell, Scala, or Elm. However, embracing functional programming is essentially adopting a new way to organize and reason about programs and their properties. This is where category theory comes in handy, supporting the structuring of software in a more reliable, predictable, and manageable form.

To appreciate the implications of category theory in functional programming, it's crucial to discuss pure functions, immutability, and statelessness. Pure functions and their composability, key tenets of category theory, form the bedrock of functional programming. Immutability, which ensures data does not change after it's created, and statelessness, which retains no record of previous interactions, both establish a deterministic coding environment. Incorporating these concepts in programming contributes to the stability, modularity, and deterministic nature of associated software.

11.4. A Quantum Jump with Category Theory

The journey of category theory does not pause here. It's also expanding its terrain in quantum computing, a revolutionary computation paradigm that harnesses quantum mechanics' peculiar properties.

The world of quantum computing is dominated by a sense of mystique due to its extremely complex working structure built on quantum states and phenomena like superposition and entanglement. Here, category theory can contribute significantly by providing a high level of abstraction that simplifies quantum programming. The typical quantum operations, which are represented using quantum gates, can be viewed as morphisms while the quantum states serve as objects within the category theory.

The concept of 'monoid' from category theory helps capture the essence of quantum protocols and algorithms such as quantum teleportation and quantum error correction. With its rigor and universality, category theory is likely to play an instrumental role in driving the new narrative of quantum computing.

11.5. Looking Forward

Evidently, category theory's role in the programming landscape is massively expanding. It's enabling better, more efficient software design, and fostering abstraction that simplifies complex concepts. From enhancing the functionality of programming languages to bridging the gap between theoretical mathematics and practical applications, its potential seems to be growing exponentially.

However, despite its criticality, category theory is often deemed esoteric due to its high level of abstraction. It is a challenge for programming communities globally to eliminate this perception and make category theory more accessible. To achieve this, they must develop tailored learning resources targeted at various user proficiency levels and foster a culture of sharing and collaboration around the topic.

As we sail through the 21st century, it is becoming increasingly evident that category theory will continue to exact its pervasive influence over the programming realm. It is destined to be at the forefront of this rapidly evolving discipline, holding the power to shape the future of code creation and optimization.

Despite the steep learning curve, the rewards reaped from comprehending and implementing category theory in programming are immense. Beyond just an abstract study of mathematics, it has the potential to be a game changer, charting a new course in the way we view, understand, and orchestrate code. With the application of category theory, programming can evolve from being a craft to an exact science, opening up unprecedented possibilities for the future.

In the grand scheme of this digitizing world, it's clear that category theory in programming is more than a mere tool—it's a paradigm that could unlock the next level of code creation and software development. The future is indeed promising for those who embark on the enlightening path from abstract mathematics to everyday coding through category theory.